Contains:

7 Lovely Words

6 Heart Mandalas

2 LOVE Typography

5 Heart Shapes

2 Animals

1 Couple

7 Designs & Doodles

2 Sweet Delights

6 Flowers

WAMA
COLORING BOOK

image on page 37: julisnegi/Fotolia.
Images on pages 5,6,9,11,13,15,16, 22, 25, 30,
32, 35, 38 and 40, used under license
from Shutterstock.com.

GANZ™
™ GANZ, Woodstock, GA 30188
ganz.com

Printed in China
978-0-9970517-2-8

I Love You
with
All My Heart